FLUTE SOUND EFFECTS

D0584821

UELI DÖRIG

BEATBOXING, CIRCULAR BREATHING, FOURTH-OCTAVE PLAYING, AND MUCH MORE!

For Irene and Hansi

Berklee Press

Editor in Chief: Jonathan Feist
Vice President of Online Learning and Continuing Education/CEO of Berklee Online: Debbie Cavalier
Assistant Vice President of Marketing and Recruitment for Berklee Media: Mike King
Dean of Continuing Education: Carin Nuernberg
Editorial Assistants: Emily Jones, Eloise Kelsey
Author Photo: Martin Cavé
Technical Flute Photographs: Etienne Nadeau-Plamondon
Cover Photo: Ueli Dörig

Recording Credits
Compositions by Evandro Gracelli and Ueli Dörig
Flute: Ueli Dörig
Guitar, Mandolin, and Voice: Evandro Gracelli
Percussion: Emilio Martins
Audio Engineering: Martin Cavé (Gatineau, Canada) and Evandro Gracelli (São Paulo, Brazil)
Audio Track "32. Beatboxing" generously provided by Greg Pattillo
Visit **www.uelidoerig.com** for more information.

ISBN 978-0-87639-164-8

Berklee
Press

1140 Boylston Street
Boston, MA 02215-3693 USA
(617) 747-2146

Visit Berklee Press Online at
www.berkleepress.com

Berklee Online
online.berklee.edu

DISTRIBUTED BY

HAL•LEONARD®
CORPORATION
7777 W. BLUEMOUND RD. P.O. BOX 13819
MILWAUKEE, WISCONSIN 53213

Visit Hal Leonard Online
www.halleonard.com

Berklee Press, a publishing activity of Berklee College of Music, is a not-for-profit educational publisher.
Available proceeds from the sales of our products are contributed to the scholarship funds of the college.

CONTENTS

ACKNOWLEDGMENTS

I'd like to acknowledge the pioneer work of Robert Dick, Bruno Bartolozzi, and Harvey Sollberger in the field of extended flute techniques. Their work and teachings are a great inspiration in my daily flute playing.

A great "thank you" goes to Wendy Rolfe and Fernando Brandão at Berklee College of Music for proofreading the manuscript and for assisting me with great advice and support.

It was a great pleasure and fantastic experience to create this book's etudes with maestro Evandro Gracelli from São Paulo, Brazil. Muito obrigado, Evandro!

This book would not exist without the wonderful work of Berklee Press staff Emily Jones, Eloise Kelsey, and their editor in chief, Jonathan Feist. Thanks guys for all your hard work and invaluable guidance.

Last but not least, I'd like to thank my beautiful wife Claudia. Je t'aime mon amour!

INTRODUCTION

Flute Sound Effects is a collection of thirty-three extended flute techniques, all fit for open- and closed-hole flutes alike. Extended techniques are a fun way to broaden our musical horizons, to push our limits, and to sharpen our skills. The techniques presented in this book are organized going from easy to hard. Some of them will be easy for you to play at the very first attempt, whereas others will require a lot of time and effort. Please be patient with yourself, make sure to respect your body's limits, and understand that becoming a better flute player is a process that takes time.

Working on these techniques will help you to enhance the knowledge of your body and your instrument. With every technique you learn, you will gain more control. The more control we have, the more freedom we have to express ourselves. In learning the material presented in this book, you will constantly add new colors to the palette of sounds available on your flute.

EXPERIMENTATION

Experimentation, a curious and playful mind, and determination are all key elements for succeeding when learning extended techniques. Most of the time, experimenting with adjustments of the embouchure, the air stream, the angle of the headjoint, dynamics, the position of the tongue, the form of the oral cavity, or the posture will fix problems that frequently occur. Experiment, and don't be shy to take notes. Use the blank fingering charts at the end of this book to track fingerings that you found through experimentation. Make copies of the blank chart, so you can use it over and over again.

This book is all about leaving your comfort zone, trying new things, and listening to the results. Your ears will always tell you if you are right or wrong, but you have to listen to them, and you have to learn to trust them.

HOW TO USE THIS BOOK

Part I of this book is about *learning* the different techniques, whereas part II is about *applying* them. Feel free to start with the techniques that seem the most interesting to you. The recorded examples provide additional guidance.

To access the accompanying audio, go to www.halleonard.com/mylibrary and enter the code found on the first page of this book. This will grant you instant access to every track. Techniques and etudes that reference audio are marked with an audio icon.

HOW TO USE EXTENDED TECHNIQUES

Using extended techniques is like using spices when cooking. If you apply the right amount of spices, your food will taste great. But always remember: Too much spice can ruin even the simplest dish! It is one thing to be capable of playing an extended technique and another to use it musically. Listen to great flute players, and pay attention to how they use extended techniques.

NOTATION OF EXTENDED TECHNIQUES

Many extended techniques do not have standardized notations. Therefore, I often provide several possible ways to notate a certain extended technique. Use your own judgment for choosing which one to use. Even better, try several and see which ones work best with other musicians. Bear in mind that the goal of music notation is to be as clear and simple as possible.

HOW TO READ THE FINGERING CHART

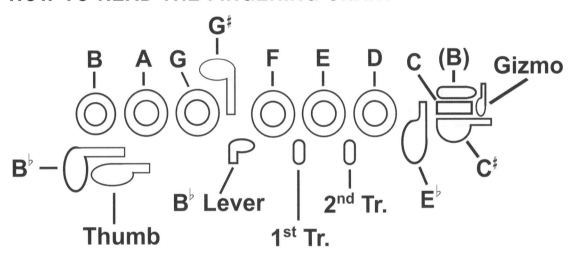

FIG. I.1. Flute Fingering Chart

We use the following conventions for fingering charts.

- A black key means that the key is pressed.

- A white key means that the key is released (not pressed).

- A grey key means that you may press the key or not (optional). Try out both options to see which one gets you better results.

The techniques discussed in chapters "12. Vibrato" and "22. Double and Triple Tonguing" are by definition "sound effects," though strictly speaking, they are not considered extended flute techniques. They have always been part of the standard (i.e., "normal," traditional) flute technique.

New extended instrumental techniques are constantly evolving, which makes this a very interesting and exciting field of study. Experiment, and think outside the box! Always keep in mind that music comes first. If a technique or an effect doesn't support or serve the music, then it's simply a gimmick.

Welcome to *Flute Sound Effects*!

PART I

Technique

1. HEADJOINT ONLY

Playing only with the headjoint facilitates experimentation with different positions, angles, air stream directions, and air speeds.

Using a Finger

The easiest way to produce different notes using only the headjoint is to simply insert a right-hand finger into the opening that usually connects the headjoint with the rest of the flute. Try sliding the pinky or the index finger inwards and outwards while blowing normally into the embouchure hole. This should create a sort of slide-whistle effect, giving you a lot of creative freedom regarding pitch and intonation. Note how using different fingers produces different results.

Using the Right Hand

Make a tunnel with your right-hand fingers, and add that tunnel to your headjoint to make it a longer tube. While blowing, lift up the right-hand fingers in order, going from pinky to index. Also, blow and put the fingers down in reversed order. Experiment with lifting your fingers at different speeds.

Another option available using your headjoint in combination with your right hand is the "gedackt/gedeckt" (German for "covered") effect. This technique comes from the way organ pipes are built. Simply cover the opening of your headjoint completely with your right hand and blow.

Using Different Air Support

Another way to produce different notes using only the headjoint is to produce whistle tones (see chapter 10) as well as a regular note with its overtone series (see chapter 18).

Rolling the Headjoint

Rolling the headjoint is also a way to change the pitch of your notes. Rolling the headjoint outwards will sharpen your notes, and rolling the headjoint inwards will flatten your notes.

This easy technique should be used as an effect, but it is very important to understand and acknowledge that (most of the time) this is not the right way to tune your notes. To play a flute in tune, one has to listen to and tune each single note individually. To properly tune a flute, one should focus on air speed, air stream direction, posture, angle of the flute, and tongue placement. It is the combination of these elements that make each single note in or out of tune.

Using Different Air Stream Directions

Changing the direction of the air stream will affect the sound quality (timbre) of the notes you play. Do not sacrifice sound quality when experimenting with different air stream directions.

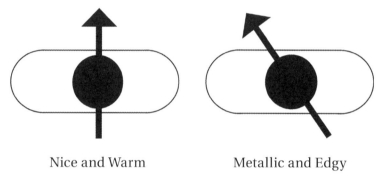

Nice and Warm   Metallic and Edgy

FIG. 1.1. Different Air Stream Directions

TIP:
You can use different air stream directions also when playing with your entire flute (normal setup).

2. HEADJOINT FINGER SLAPS

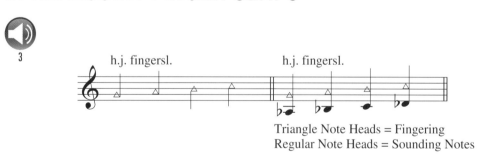

Triangle Note Heads = Fingering
Regular Note Heads = Sounding Notes

FIG. 2.1. Headjoint Finger Slaps Notation

First, try finger slaps using only the headjoint. Hold the headjoint with your left hand, and slap the tone hole with the fingertip of your right hand's middle finger. If you align the center of your fingertip perfectly with the center of the tone hole, then you should be capable of getting a fairly loud pop sound.

Next, try it with the whole flute assembled. Because your right hand is used to slap the headjoint, we are limited to the notes we are getting using only the left-hand fingers. Try getting notes at different dynamics. Note that the sound you are getting is actually a major seventh lower than the sound of the notated notes.

Place the flute on your chin (as if playing) when doing headjoint finger slaps. Then do it again, but this time with the flute off your chin. Observe how the resulting pitches are different.

TIPS:
- If you are using mouthpiece finger slaps in a recording situation, point a directional microphone towards the headjoint.
- Experiment using the headjoint finger slaps in combination with the key clapping technique (chapter 3).

3. KEY CLAPPING

Alternative Names: key clicks, key slaps, key percussion, pop

4   There are two ways to do key clapping. You can either clap the keys (rapidly close the keys of the flute) and blow through your flute at the same time, or you can clap the keys without blowing. If you choose to do key clapping without blowing, then you can also choose between covering the embouchure hole or leaving it open. Note that when covering the embouchure hole the flute will sound a major seventh below the played note.

1. Key clapping while playing a regular note:

FIG. 3.1. Key Clapping While Playing a Regular Note Notation

a. Place your fingers to play low C.

b. Leave the G key open.

c. Close the G key rapidly at the very moment you play that short accented low C.

d. Play different notes with rhythm using different fingers to clap.

2. Key clapping without blowing (open mouthpiece):

FIG. 3.2. Key Clapping Without Blowing (Open Mouthpiece) Notation

    a. Place your fingers to play low C.

    b. Leave the G key open.

    c. Close the G key rapidly at the very moment you want to do the key clap.

    d. Clap with different fingers and add rhythm.

3. Key clapping, embouchure hole closed with tongue (black rectangle = using tongue):

FIG. 3.3. Key Clapping Embouchure Hole Closed with Tongue Notation

    a. Place your fingers to play low C.

    b. Leave the G key open.

    c. Close the embouchure hole with your tongue.

    d. Close the G key rapidly at the very moment you want to do the key clap.

4. Key clapping, embouchure closed with lip (white rectangle with black dot = using lip):

FIG. 3.4. Key Clapping Embouchure Hole Closed with Lip Notation

     a. Place your fingers to play low C.

     b. Leave the G key open.

     c. Close the embouchure hole with your lower lip or with your tongue.

     d. Close the G key rapidly at the very moment you want to do the key clap.

In the above examples, I always used G as my "striker key" because it produces great results on my flute. But I strongly recommend experimentation with different striker keys in all kinds of situations. This way, you will really get to know your own instrument.

Don't limit yourself to regular fingerings either. Experiment also with irregular fingerings, and try to do two different rhythms simultaneously (polyrhythms) using your left hand and right hand independently.

Check out how changing the flute position affects the pitch of this effect. Listen to how key clapping sounds different according to the octave in which you are playing.

If you seal the embouchure hole by putting your lips around it, then you are basically adding the inside of your mouth as a resonating chamber to your flute. Do not blow; while clapping your keys, move your tongue forward and backward, and listen to how the tongue movement and position change the pitch of the key clapping. Changing the shape of your oral cavity is fun to do, as well.

You can use the blank fingering chart at the end of this book to track interesting findings.

TIPS:

- Open your throat a little bit more than you usually do, and move your mouth a tiny bit more over the embouchure hole. This will create a slightly louder sound by expanding the resonance chamber (oral cavity and flute body).

- Point a directional microphone towards the involved keys if you are using key clapping in a recording situation.

4. KEY DAMPING

5

Alternative name: key vibrato

FIG. 4.1. Key Damping Notation

Closed-Hole Flutes

By closing the keys of the flute to different degrees, we can change the notes we play quite a lot. Play a low G, and slightly move your F♯ key up and down. Do not go all the way down to F♯. You will realize that the margin, where key damping works, is quite narrow, but the better you can control this sweet spot, the more dramatic this effect will be. Once you master key damping on the low G, you should try it out on other notes in different octaves.

Open-Hole Flutes

By covering and uncovering the tone holes of an open-hole flute to different degrees, you can get similar results as if opening and closing the keys of a closed-hole flute (see previous paragraph).

Exercise

Combine key damping with other effects (e.g., flutter tongue, singing while playing, etc.).

TIP:
Use a metronome when practicing key damping.

5. LOW B

FIG. 5.1. Low B Posture. Photo by Etienne Nadeau-Plamondon.

Play a low C. Turn the end of your flute towards the upper part of your right leg. Use your leg as a damper and cover a part of your flute's end. With a little bit of practice, you will manage to lower the low C to a low B.

6. WINE CORK

6

Just like in the first lesson "Headjoint Only," closing the end of your flute with a wine cork will create a "gedackt/gedeckt" (i.e., German for "covered") effect. Experiment with blowing air at different speeds to get a multitude of different sounds using this technique.

7. TONGUE WITHOUT PITCH

FIG. 7.1. Tongue without Pitch Notation

The closed bottom end of the "V" indicates the pitch. Therefore, the first note in the above notation example is a C.

For this technique, you don't blow any air through your flute. By simply tonguing notes, your tongue will push enough air forward to produce sound. Tonguing without pitch is limited to one octave only as the upper octaves require more air support than this technique can deliver. The name of this technique is somewhat misleading, as we can actually hear a note (pitch) every time we tongue, even though we hear the sound at a very low volume.

TIPS:
- This technique can be combined with several other techniques of this book (e.g., double and triple tonguing, key clapping, key damping, pencil percussion, and others).
- Because this technique is by nature very quiet, you might want to use a microphone when using it in a recording or performance situation.

8. TONGUE CLICKS

Tongue Click
with Key Clapping

FIG. 8.1. Tongue Clicks Notation

1. **Tongue click with open embouchure hole.** Press the middle part of your tongue against the palate of your oral cavity to create a vacuum between the tongue and the palate. Now, rapidly pull down your tongue to release the vacuum. This should result in a sound we call a "tongue click." Doing this with an open mouth or with only one corner of your mouth slightly open will create different sounds. A variation of this is done via the side of the tongue instead of pulling the middle part straight down. Experiment also with different shapes of the oral cavity and compare the different results.

   If you are a movie nut, then you have seen people executing a double tongue click to give the signal to the horse to start pulling the carriage. Also, dog owners use tongue clicks to signal their dogs.

2. **Tongue click with closed embouchure hole.** In this variation of the tongue click technique, you do pretty much everything the same way as mentioned above. The only difference is that you don't open a corner of your mouth when doing the tongue click, but you put your lips around the embouchure hole to seal it. Note that your notes sound lower than notated when playing tongue clicks with a closed embouchure hole.

9. MINI FLUTE

FIG. 9.1. Mini Flute

Attach the foot joint directly to the headjoint, and your mini flute is ready to go! You can do all techniques mentioned in the previous chapters (except "5. Low B") if you close the two tone holes of the foot joint with your right hand.

TIP:

Wrap a small piece of paper around the headjoint's end to better seal the connection between the head and foot joints. Not only will this attach the two pieces tighter, but it will also diminish the danger of them accidentally falling apart.

WARNING: Do not assemble a mini flute if the connection between the two flute parts is too tight, as you might damage the headjoint.

10. WHISTLE TONES

Alternative Names: whistle notes, whistle sounds, whisper tones, flageolets

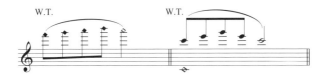

FIG. 10.1. Whistle Tones Notation

In the second notation example, the diamond shaped note indicates the fingering, whereas the regular notes indicate the sounding whistle tones.

Whistle tones are the overtone series (harmonic series) of the notes we are playing. They are a great way to warm up, because they only work if we control the airstream and embouchure well.

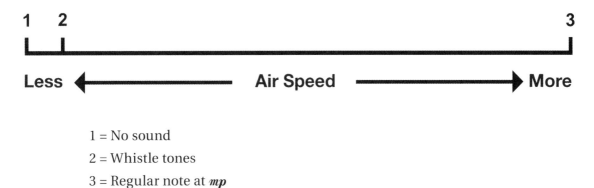

1 = No sound
2 = Whistle tones
3 = Regular note at *mp*

FIG. 10.2. Required Air Speed for Whistle Tones

A high A is a good note to start with. Play it normally first, then use less and less air. Note that *very* little air is required to produce whistle tones. The sound we are aiming for should resemble the hiss of a steaming teakettle. At first, you will probably produce fast changing whistle tones. Try to control each whistle tone by focusing on your air stream and embouchure. Your goal should be to play several different whistle tones on each regular note. The tongue position and shape are very important for this. Experiment changing the whistle tone's partials by "curling" your tongue, or by moving your tongue forward and backward, as well as up and down. Also, try keeping a little air in your cheeks, and see how this changes the sound.

TIP:
- Experiment also with irregular (made up) fingerings.
- Try playing whistle tones using the overtone series of very low notes (see chapter "18 Harmonics and Overtones").

11. AIR SOUNDS

Alternative Name: breath sounds

Exhale   Inhale   Exhale, No Headjoint   Exhale, Headjoint only   Exhale, Seal Embouchure Hole with Lips

FIG. 11.1. Inhaling and Exhaling Noises Notation

1. Inhaling and Exhaling Noises

Inhaling and exhaling noises don't include any notes being played on your flute. Breathe in and out through your flute, while surrounding the embouchure hole with your lips. Different fingerings and different air support will produce different results. The third element you can experiment with is the position of your tongue. It sounds completely different when you exhale with your tongue pressed against your upper teeth compared to when you exhale keeping your tongue in the back of your mouth. Making inhaling and exhaling noises while continuously moving your fingers can create interesting textures, too.

Inhaling and exhaling noises can easily be done for an extended period of time without stopping, which is one of the interesting aspects of this effect.

HEALTH WARNING: Stop doing this technique if you start feeling dizzy, and rest for a minute.

2. Air Sounds without Regular Notes

Alternative Names: unpitched blowing, wind sounds, wind tones

The difference between inhaling and exhaling noises and air sounds without regular notes is very small. Like the name suggests, inhaling and exhaling noises focus on breathing sounds, whereas air sounds focus more on the airy/windy quality of the sound.

FIG. 11.2. Air Sounds Notation Example

The three stripes (|||) or diamond noteheads indicate that there should only be air sounding.

There are a variety of different air sounds without regular notes that can be produced on the flute from a soft "whoosh" to a sharp "hiss." One way to create such air sounds is to put your lips around the embouchure hole while blowing through your flute. Experiment with different combinations of air speeds and fingerings. Each combination will create a different sound and texture. To add variety, produce "ssss," "ffff," and other sounds while blowing.

You can also remove the headjoint completely, hold the flute vertically, and place your lips around the barrel of the flute body. Follow the instructions in the previous paragraph, and experiment with different combinations of air speeds, fingerings, and articulations.

Another fun thing to do is to turn the headjoint around, to hold it vertically, and to blow across the connecting end of it, just as if you would blow across an open bottle. While doing this, alternate between putting down and taking off your thumb on the embouchure hole. Also, you may roll the headjoint in and out to slightly change the pitch. This effect gets even better when adding rhythm to it.

Sucking air through your flute is another way to create air sounds. By constantly inhaling (sucking) and exhaling (blowing) through the flute, you can play air sounds continuously! You can do this either with or without the headjoint being attached to your flute.

TIP:
These effects are by nature very quiet. Therefore, it is recommended that you amplify the sound with the help of a directional microphone pointed at the source of the sound.

3. Air Sounds with Regular Notes

Alternative Names: residual tones, Aeolian sounds, Soufflé (French), Soffiata (Italian)

FIG. 11.3. Air Sounds with Regular Notes Notation

Not only is it possible to mix air sounds with regular notes, but it is also possible to fade out regular notes into air sounds and vice versa. To do so, experiment with changing the embouchure, air stream pressure, and the form of the oral cavity. The more control you have over these three elements, the more flexible you will be in order to incorporate air sounds into your playing.

12. VIBRATO

FIG. 12.1. Vibrato Notation

Variation of Rate

Variation of rate refers to the speed of the vibration. It can either be described with words such as "fast vibrato" or, more precisely, with rhythmic value such as "sixteenth-note vibrato."

Variation of Width

Variation of width refers to the degree of the vibrato. The range can be from "a hint of a vibrato" to a very "dramatic and big vibrato."

Steady (or Regular) Vibrato

Steady vibrato has the same rate over time. It doesn't speed up or slow down.

Irregular Vibrato

Contrary to the steady vibrato, the *irregular vibrato* can speed up or slow down. The way musicians use irregular vibrato is a huge part of their personal sound and musical identity.

NOTE: Choosing the appropriate vibrato depends on the musical phrase you are playing.

Different Vibrato Techniques

I believe that all four vibrato techniques deserve to be explored and that they should be applied with the best musical intentions.

1. **Larynx vibrato (volume vibrato).** Play a low G. While blowing, keep saying "Ha Ha Ha …" to produce vibrato peaks. Once you can do this effortlessly, start experimenting with different vibrato speeds.

2. **Diaphragm/abdominal technique (volume vibrato).** This vibrato is established through the changing air support controlled by the diaphragm/abdomen. The peak of the vibrato happens when the air pressure is at its highest. The bottom of the vibrato happens when the air pressure is at its lowest. Again, play a low G and while blowing say forcefully "Ha Ha Ha" to produce vibrato peaks.

3. **Embouchure technique (pitch vibrato).** The vibrato is established through rolling the headjoint. Rolling the headjoint inwards will lower the pitch whereas rolling the headjoint outwards will raise the pitch. The more extremely you roll the headjoint the more extreme the width of the vibrato will be.

4. **Closing keys halfway technique (pitch vibrato).** Play a low G. Experiment with closing the F key to different degrees. When the key is almost closed, it bends the G slightly down. By moving your finger slightly back and forth in that narrow margin, you can create a vibrato. The faster you move your finger, the higher the rate of the vibrato. Try this on other notes, too.

Diaphragm/Abdominal vs. Larynx Vibrato

There is a lot of discussion regarding where the vibrato should be coming from. I have heard principal orchestra flautists defending both points of view. Personally, I use my larynx to produce most of my vibratos. My diaphragm/abdomen only kicks in when I use a more forceful and extreme vibrato, which is rarely the case.

Learn to Control Your Vibrato

Set your metronome at 60 bpm, and hold a low G. Try to pulse your vibrato to line up with every quarter-note click. Next, vibrate a bar or two of eighth notes, triplets, and sixteenth notes.

FIG. 12.2. Vibrato Exercise

TIPS:

- Do not move or shake your body while doing vibrato.

- Use a metronome when practicing steady vibrato.

- As a soloist, you have more freedom of choice when it comes to vibrato, but when playing in an orchestra or large band, it is important to choose the right kind of vibrato. Second (or third) orchestra flautists use much less vibrato than the principal player, for example (or even none). A good approach for choosing vibrato when playing with other musicians is to listen to each other and to try to blend the sound as much as possible.

13. PITCH BENDS

Alternative Name: fall-offs (when bending the notes down)

FIG. 13.1. Pitch Bends Notation

There are five different techniques to do pitch bends:

1. Turning the tone hole inward or outward (see chapter "1. Headjoint Only").
2. Altering the position of your lips, or moving the jaw, or moving the tongue.
3. Delaying the closing of the keys (see chapter "4. Key Damping").
4. Moving the head.
5. When playing with an open-hole flute, you can also slide your fingers over the open holes.

TIP:
Bending notes sometimes affects their volume. Listen carefully to how bending notes changes the volume, and adjust accordingly.

NOTES:
- One way to notate pitch bends more precisely is by writing portamenti (see the next chapter "14. Glissando and Portamento").
- A glissando is not considered to be a pitch bend because we can hear a series of different notes making up the slide (up or down). The portamento, on the other hand, can be considered to be a pitch bend as we hear only one continuously moving note (see "14. Glissando and Portamento").

14. GLISSANDO AND PORTAMENTO

The word "glissando" is Italian for sliding. Due to the flute's key work, executing glissandi (plural) can be somewhat tricky, but with some practice, we can slide upwards as well as downwards. The distance between the starting note of your glissando and the note you end on can be as little as a semi-tone, but very often, it is substantially wider. In case of a short glissando (a whole step or less) we are talking also about a "bend," whereas in the case of a long glissando, we are talking also about a "run."

NOTE: If we hear a series of notes making up the slide (going up or down), we call it a "glissando." If, on the other hand, the slide consists of only one continuously moving note, we call it a "portamento" (Italian for "carriage" or "carrying").

Short Glissando and Portamento

FIG. 14.1. Short Glissando and Portamento Notation

Short glissandi of a whole step or shorter are very similar (if not the same) to pitch bends, which is why reviewing the previous chapter, "13. Pitch Bends," will teach you how short glissandi are done.

Long Glissando and Portamento (Runs)

FIG. 14.2. Long Glissando and Portamento Notation

1. **Filling up the space with a scale (glissando).** Depending on the tempo, style, and distance between the first and the last note of the glissando, you can fill the space up with:

   - A chromatic scale (all the notes with regular fingerings available between the first and last note of the glissando), or
   - A diatonic scale (all the notes of the scale that the piece or the section of the piece is written in), or
   - Larger intervals than a minor or major second. This option is a very popular choice in fast passages.

2. **Filling up the space with a continuous slide (portamento).** A continuous slide can be produced by:

   - turning the tone hole inward or outward (see chapter "13. Pitch Bends")
   - altering the position of your lips, jaw, and/or tongue (see chapter "13. Pitch Bends")
   - delaying the closing of the keys (see chapter "4. Key Damping")
   - using microtones
   - moving your head
   - sliding your fingers when playing an open-hole flute.

15. PENCIL PERCUSSION

FIG. 15.1. Flute with Pencil. Photo by Etienne Nadeau-Plamondon.

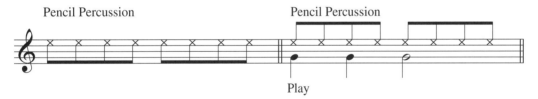

FIG. 15.2. Pencil Percussion and Playing Notation

Attach a pencil or a chopstick to your right thumb using a rubber band. Gently (!) tap the bottom side of your flute with the pencil to create rhythms.

WARNING: Do not tap your flute too hard with the pencil, as you don't want to scratch or dent your instrument. Also, do not use any metallic objects for tapping your flute, as this will most likely lead to scratches.

Exercise

South American rhythms are very effective and fun when doing pencil percussion, and they fit naturally with Latin jazz flute playing. Study Brazilian and Cuban claves, such as the son and rumba claves, and talk to drummers and percussionists about these and other fun rhythms. Additionally, you might want to check out African rhythms as well as polyrhythms (flute plays one rhythm while pencil percussion taps a different one).

16. ALTERNATE AND FALSE FINGERINGS

Alternate Fingerings

Alternate fingerings let you play regular notes using special (alternate) fingerings. The possibility of using alternate fingerings comes in handy when playing fast passages using combinations of fingerings that would usually be nearly impossible to achieve with regular fingerings. Ideally, there is no change in sound color or sound quality. Unfortunately, this is very rarely possible, as the nature of the fingering almost always influences the sound color (timbre). Alternate fingerings are also sometimes a solution for issues concerning intonation.

Avoid alternate fingerings that change the sound color, if the music you play doesn't require a change of sound color! Having said that, if you are playing at a very fast tempo and the note played with an alternate fingering sounds just for a tiny fraction of a second, then don't worry too much about it.

There is usually no need to notate alternate fingerings differently from regular notes, as they are supposed to sound exactly the same. However, if you do want to indicate false fingerings, then write "alt." for alternate fingerings and "norm." for normal fingerings on top of the notes. Should your music require a specific alternate fingering, then add a small fingering chart on top of the note(s).

False Fingerings

False fingerings are alternate fingerings that have a slightly different sound color (timbre) than the regular fingering of the same note. They are especially effective when repeatedly followed or preceded by the regular fingering of the same note.

Both alternate fingerings and false fingerings should always be played as much in tune as possible.

Contrary to alternate fingerings, false fingerings change the tone color and therefore need to be notated differently.

FIG. 16.1. False Fingering Notation

Black keys indicate keys to be pressed; white keys indicate releases (not pressed). A downward arrow means that you have to slightly roll your flute inwards to lower the note a bit.

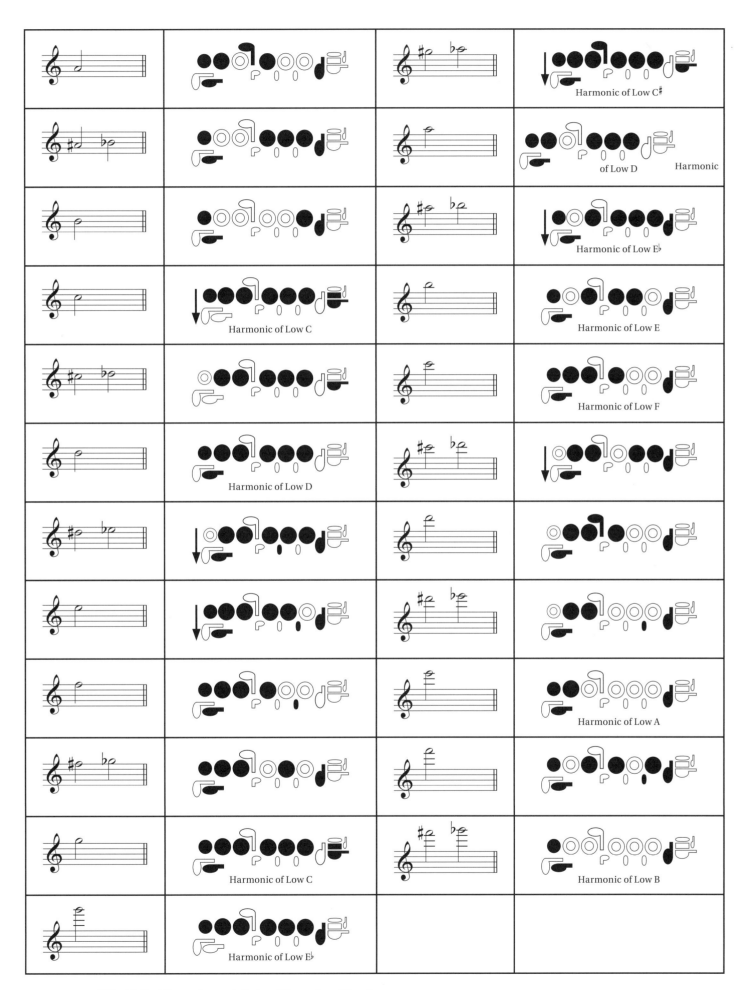

FIG. 16.2. Alternate and False Fingering Chart

Some alternate and false fingerings may work well for some people and some instruments, but not as well for others. This is partly due to the slightly different designs of many flutes. The following fingerings are meant to help you as a starting point for experimentation. In appendix A, you will find a blank fingering chart that you may copy and use to collect your own best alternate and false fingerings.

TIPS:
- Use a tuner when learning alternate and false fingerings.
- Remember the option of slightly turning your headjoint in or out to correct the tunings of these fingerings should they be a bit off.

NOTE: Some German system flutes have an open G♯ key. If you are using such a flute, you will need to adjust the fingering chart accordingly.

17. BISBIGLIANDO

Alternative Name: color trill

15   By rapidly alternating between the regular fingering of a note and a false fingering of the same note, one creates a color trill, also called *bisbigliando* (Ital.).

FIG. 17.1. Bisbigliando Notation

Use the first example if you want to avoid people mixing up the ⧣ sign with the flutter tonguing notation (see "23. Flutter Tonguing").

18. HARMONICS AND OVERTONES

FIG. 18.1. Harmonics and Overtones Notation

The upper notes with the circles are the sounding notes, whereas the lower notes indicate fingerings.

Playing harmonics and overtones is a very essential skill to master on the flute. In fact, you are actually playing a harmonic/overtone when you play a C written on the second ledger line above the staff system. Working on harmonics and overtones is a great way to increase your sound quality. Additionally, playing harmonics and overtones is also an important preliminary exercise for playing in the fourth octave (see chapter "33. Fourth-Octave Playing") and for playing alternate and false fingerings (see chapter "16. Alternate and False Fingerings).

Play a low note like a low C or a low D. Keep the same fingering and experiment with increasing the air speed to get higher and higher notes. The resulting notes are called "harmonics" or "overtones." Try to stay as relaxed as possible and avoid getting too tense when doing this.

Harmonics vs. Overtones

Harmonics and overtones are two names for the same thing with one little difference. The numbering system of the harmonics doesn't line up with the numbering system of the overtones. Unfortunately, this seems to create quite a lot of confusion. The regular note for each fingering is called the "fundamental" or "first harmonic."

Fundamental	=	1st Harmonic
1st Overtone	=	2nd Harmonic
2nd Overtone	=	3rd Harmonic
3rd Overtone	=	4th Harmonic
...	=	...

FIG. 18.2. Harmonics vs. Overtones Comparison

Harmonic and overtone series using low C as the fundamental (keep the low C fingering for all notes):

FIG. 18.3. Harmonic and Overtone Series of Low C

Harmonic and overtone series using low C♯ as the fundamental (keep the low C♯ fingering for all notes):

FIG. 18.4. Harmonic and Overtone Series of Low C♯

Harmonic and overtone series using low D as the fundamental (keep the low D fingering for all notes):

FIG. 18.5. Harmonic and Overtone Series of Low D

Harmonic and overtone series using low E♭ as the fundamental (keep the low E♭ fingering for all notes):

FIG. 18.6. Harmonic and Overtone Series of Low E♭

OBSERVATION: The same harmonic or overtone can be played using different fundamental notes (fingerings).

FIG. 18.7. Same Harmonic/Overtone Played Using Different Fundamentals

TIP:
Note how the sound color (timbre) slightly changes when playing harmonics and overtones. This effect can be exploited effectively by repeatedly and rapidly changing between a regular note and its corresponding harmonic or overtone (see "17. Bisbigliando").

HEALTH WARNING: Although the high-pitched harmonics and overtones are softer than the same high notes played with regular fingerings, consider using earplugs when practicing high harmonics and overtones. We only have one set of ears, and as musicians, we heavily depend on them.

19. ELECTRONIC EFFECTS

17

Using a microphone when playing the flute opens tons of possibilities due to electronic processing. This is especially important if you are playing electric jazz, certain types of avant-garde improvisation, or any type of popular music, which may require you to play at certain volumes and with sounds not readily available on the flute.

I recommend a basic setup that includes the following gear:

1. **Clip-on microphone and a preamp.** I prefer to use a clip-on microphone (microphone clips on flute) because it gives me the freedom to move around a little bit onstage. Choosing a microphone for your instrument is a very personal decision, which is why I recommend trying out different models and types.

2. **Volume pedal.** I use a volume pedal for three important reasons. First, I always want to have an element of control over my volume onstage. If something accidentally feeds back or is much too loud onstage, I can adjust it instantly. Second, swelling with the volume pedal is an interesting effect when used in combination with other effects. Finally, some effects, like an overdrive or distortion pedal, will increase the loudness of what comes out of the speaker, and can result in feedback without volume control.

3. **Reverb pedal.** It's likely that if you're playing with a band, the guitar, vocals, and other instruments are going to have a certain amount of reverb and sustain. The flute does not naturally have this type of sustain, and I find it effective to use a reverb to blend with the other instruments.

4. **Digital delay pedal.** A delay pedal echoes what you play within certain parameters. This allows you to fill more space without playing more, and build short segments of looped material. Many delay pedals also have a looping function, which allows you to layer sounds.

5. **Power speaker.** A 200-watt speaker is a good size to start with. You want to be able to play with enough volume without pushing your speaker to its maximum. Remember to face the speaker away from the microphone, as doing otherwise will result in feedback.

There are also a number of computer programs designed for live processing. Ableton Live, Apple's MainStage, Max/MSP, and Pure Data are currently leaders in the field, but there are also many other programs available.

TIP:
These electronic effects are widely used by electric guitar players. Talk to them about how to use these effects in a tasteful way.

20. BUZZING

18

Alternative Names: buzz-tone, trumpet sound(s), trumpet embouchure

White Note Head = Fingering
Black Note Head = Pitch

FIG. 20.1. Buzzing Notation

HEALTH WARNING: Be aware that although this effect is tons of fun, it can also be very tiresome for your lips. Always pay attention to fatigue and respect your body's limits. Overdoing buzzing can actually destroy your embouchure.

The flute can be played just like a trumpet! You can either buzz into the embouchure hole directly or you can remove the headjoint and buzz through the flute's body, holding the flute vertically. First, without your flute, press the inner parts of your lips together while blowing a sharp air stream. This should create a buzzing sound. Try to buzz different notes. Once you can buzz several notes effortlessly you are ready to experiment with combining buzzing and other effects like vibrato, flutter tongue, and hum/sing.

21. HYBRID INSTRUMENTS

A hybrid instrument is an instrument made up from parts of at least two different instruments.

"Flax"

FIG. 21.1. "Flax"

Replace the flute's mouthpiece with a soprano sax mouthpiece and neck. Wrap some painter's tape around the spot where they connect, and you are ready to go.

"Flunette"

FIG. 21.2. "Flunette"

Replace the flute's mouthpiece with the two top parts of a clarinet. The clarinet parts will be a little bit too large to fit perfectly on the flute. You can fill in the gap with some paper. Fold a small piece of paper, wrap it around the top of the flute, and put the clarinet mouthpiece back on.

"Flumpet"

21

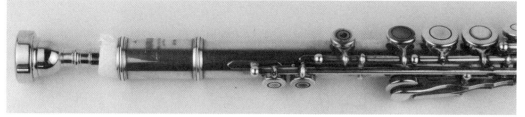

FIG. 21.3. "Flumpet"

The "flumpet" works pretty much like the "flunette." Replace the flute's mouthpiece with the mouthpiece of a trumpet. You can fill in the gap between the flute body and the trumpet mouthpiece with some paper, cork, or sponge towels.

The sound production of the "flumpet" is a bit tricky. Practice buzzing with only the trumpet mouthpiece before putting it on the flute. If you have a friend who plays the trumpet, ask for some coaching.

TIP:
All you need for further experimentation is a sound production device (mouthpiece) and a controller (instrument body with holes for different fingerings/notes).

ATTENTION: Do not injure your flute when experimenting with hybrid instruments!

22. DOUBLE AND TRIPLE TONGUING

Double and triple tonguing allow us to stop the airflow faster than single tonguing. This can be quite useful when we need to play a fast pizzicato or staccato passage. Additionally, double and triple tonguing are physically less demanding than fast single tonguing, and therefore, they cause less fatigue.

Articulation Overview

	Hard Articulation	**Soft Articulation**
Single Tonguing	Ta	Da
Double Tonguing	Ta Ka	Da Ga
Triple Tonguing	Ta Ka Ta	Da Ga Da

FIG. 22.1. Single, Double, and Triple Tonguing Articulation Overview

Double Tonguing

1. Without your flute, repeatedly sing the different articulations in the overview (one at a time). Notice how the "Ta" and "Da" are happening in the front of your oral cavity, whereas the "Ka" and "Ga" are happening in the back of your oral cavity.

2. Play a note you are very comfortable with using the articulations Ta, Da, Ka, and Ga. Pay attention to how this sounds and feels.

Ta Ta Ta Ta...　　　Da Da Da Da...　　　Ka Ka Ka Ka...　　　Ga Ga Ga Ga...

FIG. 22.2. Single Tonguing

3. Pair the following articulations: "Ta" with "Ka" and "Da" with "Ga." Play them together at a very slow tempo. When you can play them correctly, speed it up, bit by bit, until you reach a very fast tempo.

Ta Ka Ta Ka...　　　　　　　　Da Ga Da Ga...

FIG. 22.3. Double Tonguing

4. Expand your comfort zone until you cover the whole range of the flute.

Triple Tonguing

Repeat the previous steps 3 and 4 with the articulations Ta Ka Ta and Da Ga Da.

Ta Ka Ta...　　　　　　　　Da Ga Da...

FIG. 22.4. Triple Tonguing

Exercises

1. Double and triple tongue in all registers at different speeds using a metronome.

2. Double and triple tongue while playing scales and melodies.

3. Incorporate double and triple tonguing into your playing.

TIP:
Experiment with different syllables. Replace: Ta with Tu, Too, Tah; Ka with Ku, Koo, Kuh; Da with Du, Doo, Duh; Ga with Gu, Goo, and Guh. Listen to how the sound changes when using different articulations.

23. FLUTTER TONGUING

Alternative Names: Flatterzunge (German), frullato (Italian)

FIG. 23.1. Flutter Tonguing Notation

Flutter tonguing is to wind instruments what tremolo is to string instruments. There are two ways to do flutter tonguing on the flute:

1. **Rolling the tongue.** Roll the tip of your tongue, and make it flutter just like a flag in the wind. Keeping the tongue loose will make this effect easier to achieve.

2. **Vibrating the throat.** Although this is still considered flutter tonguing, we are actually not using our tongue for this technique. Just like when you are gargling water after having brushed your teeth, vibrate the uvula in the back of your throat while blowing through your flute. Note that this technique usually allows players to have more control over dynamics.

Flutter Tonguing without Pitch

Flutter tonguing can also be done while playing air sounds (see chapter "11. Air Sounds").

1. Use the following notation if the fingerings involved are important for the results:

FIG. 23.2. Flutter Tonguing without Pitch Notation

2. Use a single-line staff if the fingerings don't matter for the resulting sounds.

24. TONGUE PIZZICATO AND LIP PIZZICATO

Alternative Name: percussive tonguing

Tongue Pizzicato

FIG. 24.1. Tongue Pizzicato Notation

1. **Tongue on or between the lips.** Picture yourself squirting water from your mouth with a very narrow high-pressure jet. You wouldn't blow up your cheeks to get maximum water pressure. Imagine keeping up the pressure but blocking the water jet by putting the tip of your tongue between your lips. Now, replace the water with air, and you are almost there. Quickly draw back your tongue, and let the lips close the gap rapidly. During a fraction of a second there is air coming out of your mouth, which produces a short pop. This pop is your pizzicato sound.

2. **Tongue on the palate.** Press the tip of your tongue against the roof of your oral cavity just behind your upper teeth. Now, throw your tongue at the bottom of your mouth as quickly as possible while saying "T" (almost like a dry spit). Close your throat to trap the needed air, and compress it in your mouth before quickly releasing it when saying "T."

TIPS:
- Drop your jaw a little bit (not too much) when saying "T."
- Try to combine this effect with double and triple tonguing (see chapter "22. Double and Triple Tonguing").

Lip Pizzicato

26

FIG. 24.2. Lip Pizzicato Notation

Roll your lips firmly around your teeth and keep them pressed together while having your mouth closed. Now, to do a lip pizzicato, open your mouth as fast as you can while keeping the lips pressed around your teeth. This should result in a pop or smack sound. Lip pizzicato works best in the second octave, where you will best hear the popping sound as well as the note being played.

Another way to understand lip pizzicato is by picturing yourself kissing someone on the cheek. Just roll your lips firmly around your teeth and do a couple of smacks holding your flute in normal playing position.

25. TONGUE RAM

27

Alternative Names: tongue stop, tongue slap, "Ht," tongue thrusts

FIG. 25.1. Tongue Ram Notation

To produce tongue rams, you have to completely cover the embouchure hole with your mouth (seal the embouchure hole with your lips). Then, during a fraction of a second, blow a very sharp airstream with a lot of diaphragm support, and cut it immediately off saying "Ht." This feels very much like sneezing with the exception that your nose isn't involved at all. Experiment where to strike the outer rim of the embouchure hole with the flat part of your tongue to get the best results.

A variation of this is using the tongue ram technique (sharp airstream and saying "Ht") without closing the embouchure hole.

Yet another option is to do a tongue ram with a covered embouchure hole, but instead of saying "Ht," you rapidly push your tongue forward through the lips and into the embouchure hole. (Your tongue doesn't touch your teeth at all.)

NOTE: The notes produced using the tongue ram technique where the lips completely cover the embouchure hole sound a major seventh lower than the fingerings imply.

> **COMPOSERS:** Please specify on top of the staff if you want the embouchure hole to be closed (that's usually the case) or if you'd like the embouchure hole to be open. A black rectangle, or a white rectangle with a black circle in it, represent a closed embouchure hole, whereas a white rectangle, or a white rectangle with a white circle in it, represent an open embouchure hole. You can also write "closed embouchure hole" or "open embouchure hole" on top of the staffs (see figure 25.1).

26. JET WHISTLE

Alternative Names: air rush (A.R.), jet blow

1. Jet Whistle, Exhaling Air

FIG. 26.1. Jet Whistle Exhaling Air Notation Example 1

The special note head—commonly, a diamond, x, or triangle—indicates the fingering whereas the curved line indicates the direction of the jet whistle (here: going from high to low).

X note heads connected by a line are often used to indicate precisely where the jet whistle starts and ends.

FIG. 26.2. Jet Whistle Exhaling Air Notation Example 2

2. Jet Whistle, Inhaling and Exhaling

If both techniques, inhaling and exhaling, are used to produce jet whistle effects, express this by using different note heads.

FIG. 26.3. Jet Whistle Inhaling and Exhaling Notation

Cover the embouchure hole completely with your lips, and blow hard directly into the tone hole. The sounds you will get will heavily depend on the angle (direction) and the force of the air stream, as well as the fingerings used. Experiment with rolling the headjoint inwards or outwards as well as changing the vocalization sounds while blowing. Use "OHs," "EEHs," "AAHs," and "OOHs." The resulting sounds can vary from very soft and long wind sounds to very short, loud, and dramatic engine sounds. Note that interesting crescendo and decrescendo effects can be achieved using the jet whistle technique.

TIPS:
- Press the upper lip against the edge of the tone hole and roll the flute slightly out.
- Experiment using irregular (made-up) fingerings to expand the palette of sound colors you can get from this technique. Copy the blank fingering chart at the end of the book to log your findings.
- Once you feel comfortable using the jet whistle technique, try to combine it with vibrato, growling, and other techniques.

HEALTH WARNING: Because the jet whistle technique requires a lot of air, it is very important to pay attention to how you are feeling. Take a break if you start feeling dizzy and most importantly, avoid fainting.

27. TONE COLOR

Alternative Names: timbre, sound color

"Alternate Fingerings," "Singing While Playing," "Using Different Air Stream Directions," "Changing the Sound Production Elements," "Harmonics and Overtones," and "Facial Muscles" are all techniques that change the tone color of your notes. "Singing While Playing" and "Playing Harmonics" will be dealt with elsewhere in this book. In this chapter, I'd like to focus on the following two techniques:

1. Changing the Sound Production Elements

Experiment changing the tone color with the following techniques:

a. Change the pressure of the air stream.

b. Change the form of your oral cavity.

c. Change your embouchure. When doing so, it is normal that not only the tone color but also the tone quality changes. At a point, your tone will diminish to only air sounds. These sounds are also called "Aeolian sounds," or "soufflé" in French compositions, as well as "soffiata" in Italian music (see chapter "11. Air Sounds").

d. Use different vowels and consonants for articulation.

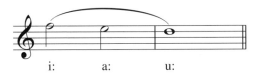

i: a: u:

FIG. 27.1. Using Different Vowels and Consonants for Articulation

e. Experiment moving your tongue around while blowing to disturb the air stream and to create turbulence.

f. Air stream direction: Do not sacrifice sound quality when experimenting with different air stream directions. I strongly encourage you to experiment with different angles and to try to memorize how they sound.

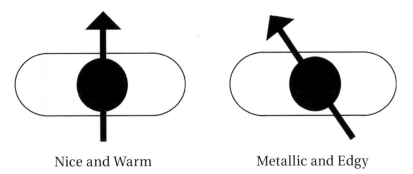

Nice and Warm   Metallic and Edgy

FIG. 27.2. Air Stream Direction

2. Facial Muscles

One thing that impresses me a lot, every time I try it out, is how the tone color changes when I force myself to open my eyes as much as possible. Somehow, this makes my notes sound brighter and facilitates playing high notes. It's a good practice habit to include checking your facial muscles every time you are controlling your posture.

HEALTH WARNING: This is a lot of fun to do, but please stop doing this before getting a headache from forcing too much.

28. GROWLING

FIG. 28.1. Growling Notation

1. **Rolling "R" technique.** In a comic book, this technique would read as an angry "Grrrr." Try to roll R's in the back of your mouth while playing your flute. Once you growl effortlessly, experiment with different speeds of the growl. Also, try out different articulations like "Trrrr," "Frrrr," "Brrrr," "Mrrrr," and others.

2. **Clearing the throat technique.** You can start practicing this technique away from your flute by humming a low note. While humming, slowly tighten your throat until it starts to rumble and growl. Once you get used to the feeling of growling using your throat, pick up your instrument, and do the same thing again while blowing through your flute.

HEALTH WARNING: This technique may be harmful to your throat if you use it over an extended period of time without taking breaks. Pay careful attention to the signals your body sends you, and stop doing growls using the clearing-the-throat technique before you get hurt.

Humming or Singing While Growling

It is possible to hum or sing while executing a growl on the flute. See chapter "29. Singing While Playing" to explore the many options available for this technique.

29. SINGING WHILE PLAYING

1. Singing and Playing the Same Notes

FIG. 29.1. Singing and Playing the Same Notes Notation

2. Singing and Playing Different Notes

FIG. 29.2. Singing and Playing Different Notes Notation

Exercises

1. Sing/hum a sustained note while playing.

FIG. 29.3. Sing/Hum a Sustained Note While Playing

TIP:

Play the sustained G on your flute first to get it in your ears. Then sing/hum the G while playing the upper part (melody).

2. Play a sustained note while singing actively.

FIG. 29.4. Play a Sustained Note While Singing Actively

TIP:

Play the upper part first with your flute to get the melody in your ears, then sing/hum it while playing a sustained G.

3. Bend notes while singing a sustained note.

Sing the highest note possible. Then, play a sustained note and start bending it down (see chapter "13. Pitch Bends").

FIG. 29.5. Bend Notes While Singing a Sustained Note

4. Sing/hum and play the same notes (unison).

FIG. 29.6. Sing/Hum and Play the Same Notes

5. Sing/hum and play the same notes in different octaves.

FIG. 29.7. Sing/Hum and Play the Same Notes in Different Octaves

TIP:
Experiment singing above as well as below the octave you are playing.

6. Sing/hum and play different notes (two independent voices). If you choose to play and sing two different notes at the same time then you have the following options:

- Parallel motion: direction and intervals are the same in both voices

- Similar motion: direction of both voices is the same but they use different intervals

- Contrary motion: one voice moves up as the other voice moves down

- Oblique motion: melodic line moves while the other voice remains at the same pitch

NOTE: Growling is a technique that is closely related to singing while playing (see chapter "28. Growling").

30. BEATBOXING

32

The one thing that sets beatboxing apart from the "Singing While Playing" technique is its purpose. The goal of beatboxing is to imitate a drum kit (or any other percussion instrument). Therefore, it is important to know the parts of a drum kit and how they sound. I highly recommend that you listen to a lot of percussion instruments and that you develop your own beatboxing vocabulary.

Try the following sounds out and listen and compare them to the sound of the real instrument. By adjusting your mouth shape and by varying the air support, you will get closer and closer to the real thing. Know that beatboxing is a very personal and individual art form, and that it's totally okay if you use different syllables to create the desired sounds.

1. Bass Drum (B.D.) = "boo" (the "oo" is tone!)

2. Floor Tom (F.T.) = "goo" or "doo"

3. Snare Drum (S.D.) = "gah"

4. Hi-Hat (H.H.) = "t" (or "tss" for open H.H.)

FIG. 30.1. Beatboxing Articulation

TIP:
Kick the air support with your diaphragm to release the syllables in the strongest way possible.

Use regular note heads for the flute playing while using x-note heads for the beatboxing.

FIG. 30.2. Beatboxing Notation

If the flute playing is busier, and having the beatboxing and the flute notes together on one staff gets too confusing, then use two-staff systems (just like piano notation). In that case, you would put the flute voice in the top staff using a treble clef while putting the beatboxing in the lower staff using a percussion clef.

Exercise

Practice the following sounds: rim shot, crash cymbal, ride cymbal, wood block, tambourine, djembe, congas, and bongos.

Once you master the beatboxing sounds effortlessly by themselves, you are ready to apply them to your flute playing:

1. Put a metronome at a slow tempo in 4/4 time. Play a note on the first beat of every measure and beatbox the rest of the measure without playing the flute. A hi-hat sound ("t") on all eighth notes starting on the second beat is a good way to start.

2. Do the same thing again, but use the hi-hat sound non-stop. Keep playing the flute on the first beat of every measure. You are now beatboxing while playing.

3. Take out your first flute book and play a very easy melody (such as a children's song). Put a bass drum sound ("boo") on the first beat of each measure. Check the bass drum sound by itself first, then together with a note, and finally, when playing the song.

4. Still playing the children's song at a slow tempo, add a second beatbox sound to it; like bass drum on beat 1 and rim shot ("kh" sound) on beat 3, for example.

5. Once this feels like a walk in a park, feel free to add more beatboxing sounds, speeding up the tempo, changing the song, or trying to beatbox when improvising.

One way to expand your beatboxing vocabulary is to try out syllables that are not related to the drum set or any other percussion instrument. By doing so, you are not technically "beatboxing" anymore, but rather, singing while playing. Syllables I have found fun to use are the hissing sounds "soh," "zah," as well as a short and percussive "too."

You may also want to review chapter "8. Tongue Clicks," which provides another percussive option that goes together well with beatboxing.

TIPS:

- Record yourself practicing beatboxing, and listen to the recordings. This will speed up the learning process tremendously.

- As beatboxing naturally relates to rhythm, using a metronome when practicing is a smart thing to do.

- Understanding basic drumming will help you to understand where to place hits on the bass drum, hi-hat, snare, etc. You can either do this by listening and analyzing music and/or by talking to drummers.

HEALTH WARNING: Always stay relaxed. If you start getting cramps in your lips, stop immediately and take a break. Be patient with yourself!

31. WHISTLING WHILE PLAYING

FIG. 31.1. Whistling While Playing

The most important technique for whistling while playing is to very gently lay the headjoint on your lower lip. If you press the headjoint too much against your lip, whistling will become impossible. On the other hand, if you only hear whistling, then press the headjoint more firmly against your lip. The margin of lip pressure is very narrow, but it is key to make this technique work.

The air-stream pressure we create when whistling is unfortunately not strong enough for playing in the mid and higher register of the flute. This means that only the first (low) octave of the flute is available for this technique.

See chapter "29. Singing While Playing" to explore more possibilities that this technique has to offer.

TIP:
Experiment with different ways of whistling.

32. CIRCULAR BREATHING

Alternative Name: recurrent breathing

FIG. 32.1. Circular Breathing Notation

Circular breathing allows you to play while simultaneously breathing in through your nose. This allows for continuous sound coming from your flute without interruption (rests, breaks).

Picture a bagpipe. Now, replace the pipe with your flute and the bag with your cheeks. As you are blowing through your instrument, you fill your cheeks with air. The moment you empty your cheeks, you quickly breathe in through your nose. During the whole process you never stop blowing. That's the theory. Now let's practice:

Go to a sink, and take as much water in your mouth as you can. At this point, your cheeks are blown up due to all the water in them. Breathe several times in and out through your nose. Relax. Continue breathing in and out, but now, start to squirt the water out in a long thin stream. You are now breathing through your nose while releasing water through your mouth. The only difference between what you are doing right now and circular breathing is that you replace the water with air.

Another great way to practice circular breathing is to use a glass half full with water, and a straw. Blow air through the straw, and blow up your cheeks. Switch from blowing air from your lungs to using the air in your cheeks. At that very moment, breathe in as much air through your nose as quickly as possible. Then immediately switch back to blowing air from your now refilled lungs, and repeat the process.

Once these preliminary exercises work effortlessly, you are ready to tackle circular breathing on your flute. The time and effort required to get this technique down varies a lot from person to person. Do not be discouraged if learning circular breathing will take you a lot of time. Start with a single note in the upper register (a high D might be a good starting point). Remember how your body felt during the preparation exercises, and try to reproduce this feeling. Relax and focus, and you will succeed.

So, here's the overall process.

1. Do the water squirting exercise.

2. Do the straw exercise.

3. Circular breathe with your flute on one note only. Start with high D, then move to other notes and expand your comfort zone. With time, try to get an even note that doesn't waver when using circular breathing.

4. Play scales while using circular breathing.

5. Incorporate circular breathing in your playing.

Only move to the next step after you've repeatedly mastered the previous exercise effortlessly!

TIP:
Take breaks if you feel dizzy. Stop immediately if you start hyperventilating!

33. FOURTH-OCTAVE PLAYING

Alternative Names: high notes, altissimo register

The fourth-octave fingerings in this book are the ones that I find easiest to play on my flute. In these charts, black keys are pressed; white keys are open. Because every flute and every player is different, *my* best fingerings might not be *your* best fingerings. Experiment, and as you find the fingerings that work best for you, track them using the blank fingering chart in the appendix.

HEALTH WARNING: Playing fourth-octave notes can be an extremely harmful process for your ears. It is of utmost importance to protect your ears with earplugs or other ear protection devices when practicing fourth-octave notes.

Because you need more tension in the lips to play the notes in the fourth octave, learning these notes could also be harmful for the relaxed embouchure. Therefore, don't practice fourth-octave notes for more than one minute at a time.

Angry neighbors might be another health hazard, but I haven't found a recipe for that problem, yet!

TIPS:
• Play the note an octave below first to get its sound in your ear. Then imagine/sing that note an octave higher.
• Release the notes by tonguing sharply.
• Sometimes, it helps rolling your flute a bit outwards.
• Open your eyes wide when playing in the fourth octave. This will favorably influence your facial muscles.
• "Kick" the air stream with your diaphragm at the same time you tongue.
• Start with my suggested fingerings and experiment by systematically adding or releasing keys, one at the time.
• Be patient with yourself.

PART I

Preparation: Third Octave Review

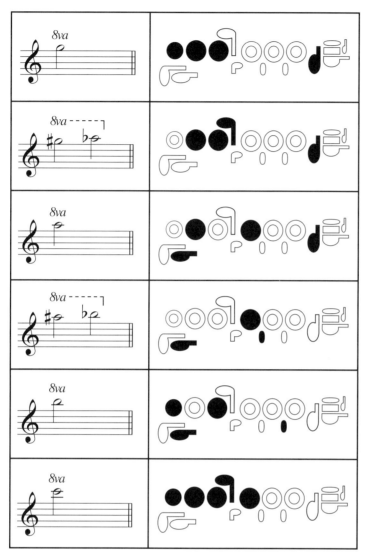

FIG. 33.1. Third Octave Fingering Chart

Fourth Octave Fingerings

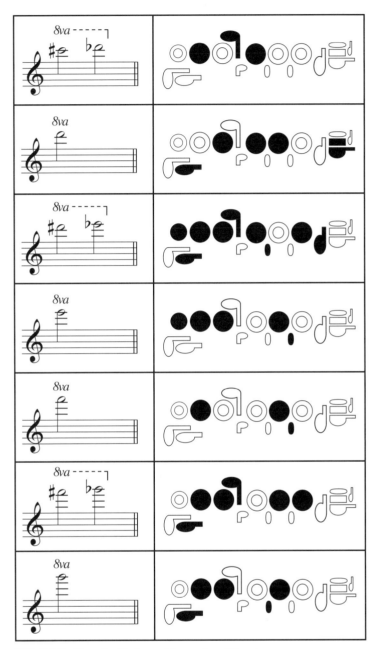

FIG. 33.2. Fourth Octave Fingering Chart

NOTE: Some German system flutes have an open G♯ key. If you are using such a flute, you will need to adjust the fingering chart accordingly.

Feel free to expand your range above the fourth-octave G through experimentation, and track your findings in the blank fingering chart in the appendix.

PART II

Etudes

The following etudes are a playground where you can apply the techniques described in part I. Each etude includes many extended techniques. However, *do not feel compelled to play all of the indicated techniques every time you play an etude!* Instead, try some of the techniques while omitting the others, to suit your musical taste. This leaves you with numerous combinations and variations for each etude.

These works were co-composed with Brazilian composer Evandro Gracelli, and they reference various Brazilian styles. Although vibrato and trills are important elements of Brazilian flute playing, they are not traditionally included in the music notation. Feel free to add both of them to your taste.

Also, try improvising freely over the etudes, using any additional techniques from part I that are not notated here (e.g., beatboxing).

1. "AFROGIL"

"AfroGil" is based on the Brazilian groove "afoxé." The air sounds at the beginning of the etude should resemble the sound of waves hitting the beach. They set up a "dreamy" vacation mood that gets carried throughout the song.

34, 35

AFROGIL

By Evandro Gracelli
and Ueli Dörig

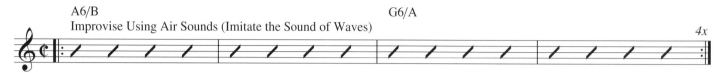

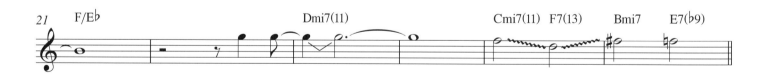

2. "BOSSA MINEIRA"

36, 37

"Bossa Mineira" is inspired by the beautiful work of prominent Brazilian singer-songwriter and guitarist Milton Nascimento. This more delicate etude is a ballad, so be extra-careful not to disturb it by overusing the extended techniques.

BOSSA MINEIRA

By Evandro Gracelli
and Ueli Dörig

3. "FREVO"

38, 39

"Frevo" is based on a frenetic northeastern Brazilian rhythm. The main focus of this etude is double tonguing. Alternatively, you could play the melody first using eighth notes and then double-tongued sixteenth notes on the repetition.

FREVO

By Evandro Gracelli
and Ueli Dörig

4. "HERMETIC"

40, 41

"Hermetic" is a tribute to beloved Brazilian composer and multi-instrumentalist Hermeto Pascoal. When tonguing without pitch at the beginning of the etude, try to become a member of the band, and to fit in as much as possible. In the "harmonics" section, feel free to improvise using different harmonics and rhythms.

HERMETIC

5. "MOACIR"

42, 43

"Moacir" is inspired by the wonderful work of Brazilian master composer, multi-instrumentalist, and music educator Moacir Santos. In the second section of this etude, make sure that you can hear the flute's air sounds and the whistling, simultaneously. At the end, stop improvising with the headjoint early enough that you have sufficient time to put it back on the flute's body.

MOACIR

By Evandro Gracelli
and Ueli Dörig

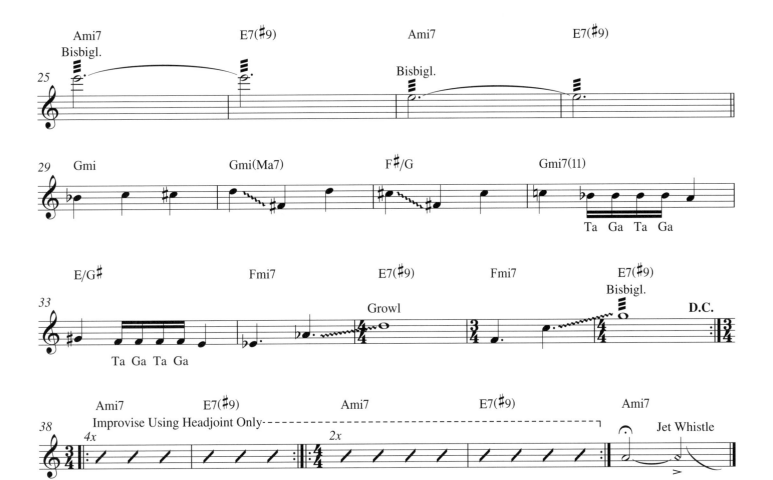

6. "SAMBIN"

44, 45

"Sambin" is a fast samba. Keep in mind that this is dance music, and use the extended techniques to support this. Experiment and improvise with other sound effects from part I.

SAMBIN

By Evandro Gracelli
and Ueli Dörig

AFTERWORD

It takes courage to leave one's comfort zone, but by doing so, we gain new experiences and move forward in our personal musical development. It is my hope that *Flute Sound Effects* is a good companion on your musical journey. Keep your eyes and ears open for the possibilities evolving extended flute techniques offer, and try to include these sounds in your daily playing. Music is a living thing, and it lives through the breath you blow through your flute.

Thank you very much, and good luck in your future musical endeavors.

—Ueli

APPENDIX A

Fingering Charts

BLANK FINGERING CHART A

BLANK FINGERING CHART B

APPENDIX B

Resources

RECOMMENDED READING

Brandão, Fernando. *Brazilian and Afro-Cuban Jazz Conception*. Rottenburg: Advance Music, 2006.

Dick, Robert. *Tone Development Through Extended Techniques: Flute Etudes and Instruction*. St. Louis: Lauren Keiser Music Publishing, 2008.

Mazur, Andreas. *Das Pars-pro-Toto Spiel*. Erzhausen: Musikverlag Zimmermann, 2003.

Moyse, Marcel. *De La Sonorite: Art et Technique*. Paris: Alphonse Leduc, 1934.

Offermans, Wil. *For the Contemporary Flutist*. Erzhausen: Musikverlag Zimmermann, 1997.

Wilcocks, Gerda Reinette. *Improving tone production on the flute with regards to embouchure, lip flexibility, vibrato, and tone color, as seen from a classical music perspective*. MMus thesis. University of Pretoria, Pretoria, 2006.

Wye, Trevor. *Practice Book for the Flute: Volume 1—Tone*. London: Novello, 1980.

Zalba, Javier. *Flute Soneando: The Flute in Popular Cuban Music*. Rottenburg: Advance Music, 2000.

RECOMMENDED LISTENING

Extended Flute Techniques

Matthias Ziegler

Wil Offermans

Greg Pattillo

Jazz Flute

Rahsaan Roland Kirk

Herbie Mann

Hubert Laws

Ian Anderson

Latin Flute

Nestor Torres

Dave Valentin

Orlando "Maraca" Valle

Richard Egües

ABOUT THE AUTHOR

Photo by Martin Cavé

Ueli Dörig is a multi-instrumentalist, music educator, and performing artist. He grew up in Rorschach, Switzerland where he got a bachelor degree in education. After some years of teaching in public school and serving as a Swiss Army musician, he went on to study at Berklee College of Music in Boston, where he graduated with distinction in both performance and jazz composition. Since 2007, he has lived in Canada's capitol region (Ottawa/Gatineau). Ueli Dörig is the author of *Saxophone Sound Effects* (Berklee Press 2012), *Trumpet Sound Effects* (Berklee Press 2014, co-authored with Craig Pedersen), and several other music books. For more information, visit **www.uelidoerig.com**.

More Fine Publications
from BERKLEE PRESS

GUITAR

BEBOP GUITAR SOLOS
by Michael Kaplan
00121703 Book...........................$14.99

BERKLEE BLUES GUITAR SONGBOOK
by Michael Williams
50449593 Book/CD..............................$24.99

BLUES GUITAR TECHNIQUE
by Michael Williams
50449623 Book/CD..............................$24.99

BERKLEE GUITAR CHORD DICTIONARY
by Rick Peckham
50449546 Jazz – Book.........................$10.99
50449596 Rock – Book.........................$12.99

BERKLEE JAZZ STANDARDS FOR SOLO GUITAR
by John Stein
50449653 Book/CD..............................$19.99

THE CHORD FACTORY
by Jon Damian
50449541 Book.................................$24.95

CREATIVE CHORDAL HARMONY FOR GUITAR
by Mick Goodrick and Tim Miller
50449613 Book/CD..............................$19.99

FUNK/R&B GUITAR
by Thaddeus Hogarth
50449569 Book/CD..............................$19.95

GUITAR CHOP SHOP – BUILDING ROCK/METAL TECHNIQUE
by Joe Stump
50449601 Book/CD..............................$19.99

INTRODUCTION TO JAZZ GUITAR
by Jane Miller
00125041 Book/Online Audio.............$19.99

JAZZ IMPROVISATION FOR GUITAR
by Garrison Fewell
A Harmonic Approach
50449594 Book/CD..............................$24.99
A Melodic Approach
50449503 Book/CD..............................$24.99

A MODERN METHOD FOR GUITAR*
by William Leavitt
Volume 1: Beginner
00137387 Book/Online Video........... $34.99
*Other volumes, media options, and supporting songbooks available.

PLAYING THE CHANGES: GUITAR
by Mitch Seidman and Paul Del Nero
50449509 Book/CD $19.95

THE PRACTICAL JAZZ GUITARIST
by Mark White
50449618 Book/CD..............................$19.99

THE PRIVATE GUITAR STUDIO HANDBOOK
by Michael McAdam
00121641 Book...........................$14.99

BASS

BASS LINES
Fingerstyle Funk
by Joe Santerre
50449542 Book/CD $19.95
Metal
by David Marvuglio
00122465 Book/Online Audio.............$19.99
Rock
by Joe Santerre
50449478 Book/CD $19.95

FUNK BASS FILLS
by Anthony Vitti
50449608 Book/CD $19.99

INSTANT BASS
by Danny Morris
50449502 Book/CD $14.95

READING CONTEMPORARY ELECTRIC BASS
by Rich Appleman
50449770 Book.................................$19.95

DRUMS

BEGINNING DJEMBE
by Michael Markus & Joe Galeota
00148210 Book/Online Video $16.99

DOUBLE BASS DRUM INTEGRATION
by Henrique De Almeida
00120208 Book.................................$19.99

DRUM SET WARM-UPS
by Rod Morgenstein
50449465 Book.................................$12.99

DRUM STUDIES
by Dave Vose
50449617 Book.................................$12.99

EIGHT ESSENTIALS OF DRUMMING
by Ron Savage
50448048 Book/CD $19.99

PHRASING: ADVANCED RUDIMENTS FOR CREATIVE DRUMMING
by Russ Gold
00120209 Book.................................$19.99

WORLD JAZZ DRUMMING
by Mark Walker
50449568 Book/CD $22.99

PIANO/KEYBOARD

BERKLEE JAZZ KEYBOARD HARMONY
by Suzanna Sifter
00138874 Book/Online Audio............$24.99

BERKLEE JAZZ PIANO
by Ray Santisi
50448047 Book/CD $19.99

CHORD-SCALE IMPROVISATION FOR KEYBOARD
by Ross Ramsay
50449597 Book/CD..............................$19.99

CONTEMPORARY PIANO TECHNIQUE
by Stephany Tiernan
50449545 Book/DVD $29.99

HAMMOND ORGAN COMPLETE
by Dave Limina
50449479 Book/CD $24.95

JAZZ PIANO COMPING
by Suzanne Davis
50449614 Book/CD $19.99

LATIN JAZZ PIANO IMPROVISATION
by Rebecca Cline
50449649 Book/CD $24.99

SOLO JAZZ PIANO – 2ND ED.
by Neil Olmstead
50449641 Book/CD............................$39.99

VOICE

BELTING
by Jeannie Gagné
00124984 Book/Online Media............$19.99

THE CONTEMPORARY SINGER – 2ND ED.
by Anne Peckham
50449595 Book/CD $24.99

TIPS FOR SINGERS
by Carolyn Wilkins
50449557 Book/CD.............................$19.95

VOCAL TECHNIQUE
featuring Anne Peckham
50448038 DVD...................................$19.95

VOCAL WORKOUTS FOR THE CONTEMPORARY SINGER
by Anne Peckham
50448044 Book/CD.............................$24.95

YOUR SINGING VOICE
by Jeannie Gagné
50449619 Book/CD $29.99

WOODWINDS/BRASS

FAMOUS SAXOPHONE SOLOS
arr. Jeff Harrington
50449605 Book...................................$14.99

FLUTE SOUND EFFECTS
by Ueli Dörig
00128980 Book/Online Audio............$14.99

THE SAXOPHONE HANDBOOK
by Douglas D. Skinner
50449658 Book...................................$14.99

SAXOPHONE SOUND EFFECTS
by Ueli Dörig
50449628 Book/CD $15.99

TRUMPET SOUND EFFECTS
by Craig Pedersen and Ueli Dörig
00121626 Book/Online Audio.............$14.99

ROOTS MUSIC/STRINGS

BEYOND BLUEGRASS

Beyond Bluegrass Banjo
by Dave Hollander and Matt Glaser
50449610 Book/CD $19.99

Beyond Bluegrass Mandolin
by John McGann and Matt Glaser
50449609 Book/CD $19.99

Bluegrass Fiddle and Beyond
by Matt Glaser
50449602 Book/CD $19.99

EXPLORING CLASSICAL MANDOLIN
by August Watters
00125040 Book/Online Media $19.99

FIDDLE TUNES ON JAZZ CHANGES
by Matt Glaser
00120210 Book/Online Audio $16.99

THE IRISH CELLO BOOK
by Liz Davis Maxfield
50449652 Book/CD $24.99

JAZZ UKULELE
by Abe Lagrimas, Jr.
00121624 Book/Online Audio $19.99

BERKLEE PRACTICE METHOD

GET YOUR BAND TOGETHER
With additional volumes for other instruments, plus a teacher's guide.

Bass
by Rich Appleman, John Repucci and the Berklee Faculty
50449427 Book/CD $14.95

Drum Set
by Ron Savage, Casey Scheuerell and the Berklee Faculty
50449429 Book/CD $14.95

Guitar
by Larry Baione and the Berklee Faculty
50449426 Book/CD $16.99

Keyboard
by Russell Hoffmann, Paul Schmeling and the Berklee Faculty
50449428 Book/CD $14.95

WELLNESS

MANAGE YOUR STRESS AND PAIN THROUGH MUSIC
by Dr. Suzanne B. Hanser and Dr. Susan E. Mandel
50449592 Book/CD $29.99

MUSICIAN'S YOGA
by Mia Olson
50449587 Book $14.99

THE NEW MUSIC THERAPIST'S HANDBOOK – SECOND ED.
by Dr. Suzanne B. Hanser
50449424 Book $29.95

MUSIC THEORY/EAR TRAINING/ IMPROVISATION

BEGINNING EAR TRAINING
by Gilson Schachnik
50449548 Book/CD $16.99

THE BERKLEE BOOK OF JAZZ HARMONY
by Joe Mulholland & Tom Hojnacki
00113755 Book/CD $24.99

BERKLEE MUSIC THEORY – 2ND ED.
by Paul Schmeling
Rhythm, Scales Intervals
50449615 Book/CD $24.99
Harmony
50449616 Book/CD $22.99

BLUES IMPROVISATION COMPLETE
by Jeff Harrington
50449425 C Treble Instruments:
Book/CD $22.99
Also available for B♭ and E♭ instruments.

A GUIDE TO JAZZ IMPROVISATION
by John LaPorta
50449439 C Instruments:
Book/CD $19.95
Also available for B♭, E♭, and bass clef instruments.

IMPROVISATION FOR CLASSICAL MUSICIANS
by Eugene Friesen with Wendy M. Friesen
50449637 Book/CD $24.99

REHARMONIZATION TECHNIQUES
by Randy Felts
50449496 Book $29.95

MUSIC BUSINESS

HOW TO GET A JOB IN THE MUSIC INDUSTRY – 3RD EDITION
by Keith Hatschek with Breanne Beseda
00130699 Book $27.99

MAKING MUSIC MAKE MONEY
by Eric Beall
50448009 Book $26.95

MUSIC INDUSTRY FORMS
by Jonathan Feist
00121814 Book $14.99

MUSIC MARKETING
by Mike King
50449588 Book $24.99

PROJECT MANAGEMENT FOR MUSICIANS
by Jonathan Feist
50449659 Book $27.99

THE SELF-PROMOTING MUSICIAN – 3RD EDITION
by Peter Spellman
00119607 Book $24.99

MUSIC PRODUCTION & ENGINEERING

AUDIO MASTERING
by Jonathan Wyner
50449581 Book/CD $29.99

AUDIO POST PRODUCTION
by Mark Cross
50449627 Book $19.99

MIX MASTERS
by Maureen Droney
50448023 Book $24.95

UNDERSTANDING AUDIO
by Daniel M. Thompson
50449456 Book $24.99

HAL•LEONARD®
CORPORATION
7777 W. BLUEMOUND RD. P.O. BOX 13819 MILWAUKEE, WI 53213

Prices subject to change without notice. Visit your local music dealer or bookstore, or go to **www.berkleepress.com**

SONGWRITING, COMPOSING, ARRANGING

ARRANGING FOR HORNS
by Jerry Gates
00121625 Book/Online Audio $19.99

ARRANGING FOR LARGE JAZZ ENSEMBLE
by Dick Lowell and Ken Pullig
50449528 Book/CD $39.95

BEGINNING SONGWRITING
by Andrea Stolpe with Jan Stolpe
00138503 Book/Online Audio $19.99

COMPLETE GUIDE TO FILM SCORING – 2ND ED.
by Richard Davis
50449607 .... $27.99

JAZZ COMPOSITION
by Ted Pease
50448000 Book/CD $39.99

MELODY IN SONGWRITING
by Jack Perricone
50449419 Book/CD $24.95

MODERN JAZZ VOICINGS
by Ted Pease and Ken Pullig
50449485 Book/CD $24.95

MUSIC COMPOSITION FOR FILM AND TELEVISION
by Lalo Schifrin
50449604 Book $34.99

MUSIC NOTATION
PREPARING SCORES AND PARTS
by Matthew Nicholl and Richard Grudzinski
50449540 Book $16.99

MUSIC NOTATION
THEORY AND TECHNIQUE FOR MUSIC NOTATION
by Mark McGrain
50449399 Book $24.95

POPULAR LYRIC WRITING
by Andrea Stolpe
50449553 Book $14.95

SONGWRITING: ESSENTIAL GUIDE
Lyric and Form Structure
by Pat Pattison
50481582 Book $16.99
Rhyming
by Pat Pattison
00124366 2nd Ed. Book $17.99

SONGWRITING STRATEGIES
by Mark Simos
50449621 Book/CD $22.99

THE SONGWRITER'S WORKSHOP
Harmony
by Jimmy Kachulis
50449519 Book/CD $29.95
Melody
by Jimmy Kachulis
50449518 Book/CD $24.95

AUTOBIOGRAPHY

LEARNING TO LISTEN: THE JAZZ JOURNEY OF GARY BURTON
by Gary Burton
00117798 Book $27.99

1215